Haunted
Temecula Valley

**BOOK ONE:
GHOSTS IN UNEXPECTED
PLACES**

David J. Schmidt

Haunted Temecula Valley
Book One: Ghosts in Unexpected Places

ISBN: 9798357233257

Cover photo by David J. Schmidt.

For more information, see:
www.HolyGhostStories.com

"All houses wherein men have lived and died
Are haunted houses. Through the open doors
The harmless phantoms on their errands glide,
With feet that make no sound upon the floors.

We meet them at the doorway, on the stair,
Along the passages they come and go,
Impalpable impressions on the air,
A sense of something moving to and fro."
-Haunted Houses," by Henry Wadsworth Longfellow

Table of Contents

Introduction

"You left the bodies and you only moved the headstones! You only moved the headstones! Why? Why?!"
 -Poltergeist, 1982

When we imagine ghostly encounters, we usually picture a quintessential "haunted place": some old mansion built centuries ago, with portraits of its former owners that seem to stare at you as you pass; an historic building whose wooden floors creak menacingly; a place filled with cobwebs and musty smells.

We don't typically think of a brand new tract home, a modern strip mall, or a high school campus. Everyday suburban locations like these don't get "haunted," do they?

When I moved to Temecula as a teenager in the 1990s, the town felt like the last place to find ghost stories. It all seemed terribly bland and devoid of personality. "Suburbia Hell," we called it, nothing but mass-produced chain restaurants, cookie-cutter convenience stores, and tract homes galore. Sure, we had our Old Town, but even those old-timey buildings were mostly modern recreations of an imagined past, closer to Disneyland than any historic Western town. I thought of Temecula as "Nowhere, USA," disconnected from history, a sterile place with no roots or character of its own.

Then I started to hear the ghost stories.

They popped up in the most unexpected places, including my own high school campus. Beneath the veneer of mass-produced tract homes and strip malls, ancient history lay bubbling and broiling. Temecula started to look less like *Leave it to Beaver* and more like the 1982 horror film, *Poltergeist.* Beneath the prosperous suburban development, something ancient was lurking, something that refused to be forgotten. The protagonists in *Poltergeist* eventually learn that their housing development isn't built on "empty" land at all—a massive graveyard lies beneath it, skeletons and coffins trampled upon, restless spirits provoked.

During my high school years in Temecula, I heard accounts of poltergeist phenomena in the most ordinary places. Rumors of "Native American burial grounds" abounded throughout the region. Although I left town and went off to college, I never forgot those tales. Many years later, I came back to revisit the ghosts, hoping to find enough for a short pamphlet-sized book. Instead, I found my hometown to be immensely rich in paranormal lore, enough to fill several volumes. And so this series was born.

Welcome to the haunted Temecula Valley.

* * * *

The books in this series will cover a variety of topics and genres of supernatural lore from the Temecula Valley. As I quickly discovered, ghost stories are just the tip of the iceberg. This region is steeped in ancient mysteries: shamanism, enigmatic rock art, sacred canyons and forbidden valleys. For centuries, witnesses have spotted UFOs and strange lights in the sky. Local legends tell of hairy apelike creatures, lake monsters, and beasts beyond description.

Then, of course, there are the ghosts: full-bodied apparitions, "noisy ghosts," mischievous haunts, and foreboding presences. They haunt every corner of this valley, from our schools and homes to the remote country highways and old train tracks. In collecting these stories, I have expanded the definition of "Temecula Valley" as broadly as possible, including the nearby towns of Murrieta, Fallbrook, Lake Elsinore, and beyond. There is historical precedent for this, as author Tom Hudson explains in his seminal book, *A Thousand Years in Temecula Valley*. In Chapter 23, titled "Beyond the City Limits," he explains:

No history of Temecula valley would be complete without at least a background account of neighboring communities that have played a part in the making of that history. The name Temecula implies something more than just one village, or just one valley for that matter. Its connotation is wider than that. In fact, many first settlers referred to the entire surrounding countryside as "The Temecula."

Hudson includes many nearby areas—Warner Springs, Aguanga, Fallbrook, Rainbow Valley, Lake Elsinore, Wildomar, Murrieta, Palomar Mountain, and Pala—in his book on "the Temecula," and I have chosen to do the same. A handful of stories come from places even further away, mostly because they were just too haunting and eerie to pass up.

As you read the volumes of this series, please feel free to skip around. You won't be lost if you start on Book 8 or 9 without reading this first installment. You may feel particularly drawn to tales from a certain region like Murrieta, Lake Elsinore, or Temecula's own Old Town neighborhood. You may be more interested in cryptids and strange creatures, rather than ghost stories; you may be partial to UFOs or desert mysteries. I hope you enjoy every book, including this first volume.

Join me as we explore the hidden, haunted corners of this southern California town. As you read, you may discover that there is much more to Temecula than meets the eye. You may be inspired to dig deeper into the lore of your own neighborhood or place of work.

You just might find a ghost or two of your own.

-David J. Schmidt
2022

CHAPTER 1
The Hangman's Tree in the Steakhouse

Corner of Jefferson Avenue and Overland Drive

Dane was the last employee left in the restaurant that night. He hurried to finish setting tables in the back of the dining area for the following day. Eerily quiet, the only noise was that of the silverware shuffling in the plastic tub he carried. The normally cliché Western decor felt almost sinister in the solitary silence; the dark wood paneling seemed to absorb all light. When Dane knelt on the red leather booths to carefully lay out the silverware, the seats groaned softly. Every so often, he glanced over his shoulder, with the odd feeling that someone was watching him.

When Dane finished setting the long table in the center of the dining room, it was time to clock out and go home. He headed back into the kitchen, walking through the Western saloon-style swinging doors, and put away the empty plastic tub. When he returned to the dining room, he stopped in his tracks. A high-pitched gasp came from the back of his throat.

The silverware that he'd so carefully laid out on each table now lay on the long central table, stacked in a haphazard pile. Dane ran out the back door, swearing never to take another night shift again.

I worked in this same restaurant in the year 2000, shortly after finishing high school. Within my first week, I started to hear stories about the ghosts. According to Dane and the other employees, the entire restaurant was built on the place where many people suffered a long, painful death.

* * * *

The haunted restaurant was one of the oldest in town, originally established in 1986 under the name "Tony's Spunky Steer." When I worked there, the name had recently been changed to RJ's Sizzlin' Steer. The place looked unremarkable from the outside, located at the back end of a strip mall on Jefferson Avenue. Inside, its decorations evoked the feel of the Old West, with wood-paneled walls decorated with lassoes, saddles, and paintings of cowboys and Native Americans. Even the light fixtures were designed as old-fashioned kerosene lanterns.

Perhaps it was this Old West atmosphere that convinced the ghosts to stick around. As I got to know my coworkers, I learned that nearly everyone had encountered some sort of paranormal phenomenon.

The first one I heard of came from a dishwasher who was so jumpy I learned to avoid making any sudden movements around him. Whenever I walked up on him alone, he would shout and drop whatever he was holding. "Why is Guillermo so nervous around me?" I asked a waitress one day. "I always try to act friendly."

"He's that way with everybody. You'll have to ask him yourself," she said. "He can tell you his story… If he wants to."

I approached Guillermo one day and asked if anything was wrong. He stared off into space for a moment. "It's just that… I don't like to work here alone," he said at last. "Not after what happened."

He told me he had been washing dishes late one night with the quiet, empty kitchen to his back. Suddenly, he felt a hand tap him on the shoulder.

"It was hard," he said. "Like this." He patted me roughly with an open-palm. "Like someone really wants to get your attention."

Guillermo had whirled around, expecting to see a coworker smiling and laughing at his prank. Not a soul stood in the empty kitchen.

It wasn't just employees like Guillermo and Dane who encountered ghosts. Even the owner, Cindy, told me about them. One Friday night after closing, she and her co-managers sat in the lobby, smoking and having a few beers. They had been laughing and joking, when a mug of beer suddenly flew off the table and shattered against the wall.

"It didn't just fall or slip off," Cindy told me. "Nobody knocked it off; none of us were even near it. The mug raised straight up off the table, hovered in the air for a second, then flew across the room."

The most discomforting part of the entire restaurant, however, was the dining room where Dane had found the silverware piled up that night. That smaller dining room, located at the very back of the restaurant, seemed to be perpetually darker than the rest of the place. When Dane told me his story, I asked if it was possible that it had all been a practical joke by a coworker.

"I wondered that too, David. All the doors to the restaurant were locked, though. I could see clearly that there were no cars in the parking lot. Plus, I was only out of the dining room for a second, and I would have heard someone come in. Believe me, I tried to think up some logical explanation for it. I really wanted to. But I couldn't."

Dane was not the only employee to find something strange in that back room. I chatted with a line cook who was originally from a small town in Veracruz, southern Mexico. He swore that he walked into that back dining room one night after closing, and saw a little girl standing in the middle of the floor.

"She was dressed in old-fashioned clothing," he said. "I grew up watching old dubbed episodes of that gringo TV show, *Little House on the Prairie,* and she looked just like those people. She had on an old-fashioned floral print dress with a bonnet."

The girl stared straight into his eyes, he said, not moving. He stared back for a few seconds before the girl vanished into thin air.

"Now I'm from Veracruz. We've got all sorts of frightening things there: ghosts, monsters, black magic. We have a whole town, Catemaco, where people go to practice witchcraft. I thought I'd be getting *away* from all that stuff when I came up here to the States. And then I see this little ghost girl, right here in the restaurant!"

Even people who didn't work at the restaurant felt a strange vibe in that back dining room. Customers avoided it without any clear reason, asking to be seated elsewhere. There was no logical reason to stay out. In fact, I found the smaller dining room cozy and intimate, far from the noise of the kitchen and the bustle of the front desk. And yet, customers avoided it.

It seemed the room had a way of attracting negative, dark energy into itself. During the restaurant's yearly Christmas party, that was always where the drama happened. While most of the staff partied, danced and laughed in the main dining room, that dark back room seemed to suck all that happiness away, wicking it up hungrily. Lifelong friends who went back there found themselves fighting; waitresses went there and broke down crying for no clear reason.

I asked my coworkers if they had any theories about why the place was haunted. Many would point across the parking lot, to the old adobe house that still stood on its original site. The González adobe was one of the oldest houses still standing in Temecula, evidence that this part of town had been settled for many years.

"The real reason this place is haunted, though," a busboy told me, "is because of what *used* to be here. At the back end of the property—right where that smaller dining room is—that was where the hangman's tree used to be. In the Old West days, they executed criminals there."

Was the root cause, then? Did the vengeful spirits who died a long, painful death at the end of a rope still cling to this place, tormenting the living?

The idea of a haunted house sitting over the site of a hangman's tree is nothing new. Years after I moved away from Temecula to San Diego, I learned that one of the city's most famous haunted spots has a similar story.

The Whaley House in Old Town San Diego attracts ghost hunters from across the globe, billed as "America's most haunted house." According to local lore, the old hanging tree once stood where the Whaleys later built the parlor to their home, directly on the spot of the doorway between rooms. Famous San Diegans were executed there, from boat thief Yankee Jim to insurrectionist Bill Marshall. Folks say that if you walk beneath that archway, you feel something constricting around your neck.

On the other hand, some San Diego historians say that it's all apocryphal, that the hangman's tree never stood near that house. This made me wonder about the stories of the Sizzlin' Steer. When researching for this book, I made it my first question to investigate: did they really hang people on the site of the restaurant?

CHAPTER 2
The Haunted Preschool

Corner of Jefferson Avenue and Overland Drive

Twenty years after I had worked at the steakhouse, I went back to Temecula to investigate. I wanted to learn the truth about the hangman's tree. First, though, I decided to visit the old restaurant, to see if anyone still experienced the ghosts.

The place had changed hands at some point, now known as Mantra Indian Restaurant. When I first walked in the front door, I was struck by the sense that one ghost was definitely still there: the ghost of the old steakhouse. Despite the new owners, the decor inside was still nearly identical: Old West-style wood paneling on the walls, wooden barn frames in the doorways. A few modern decorations from India looked incongruous set into that background.

I introduced myself to the employee behind the cash register, a young man with a heavy Indian accent. I told him that I used to work there, and we talked about mundane topics for a while. Finally, I dropped the question: "Hey, I was wondering about something… Do strange things still happen here?"

He looked at me suspiciously.

"No," he replied without cracking a smile. "No strange. Only banquet."

I thought there may have been some language comprehension issues. "I was wondering about ghosts… We used to say this place was haunted."

"No, no ghosts."

"How about that back room?" I pointed toward the smaller dining room where Dane had experienced the poltergeist silverware pile. "Is that still used for dining?"

"Yes. Back room. Special event. Banquet."

"And nothing strange happens there?"

"No, no, nothing strange. Only dinner party. Banquet."

Finally, I thanked him and left. I felt downtrodden. The ghosts seemed to have left along with the steaks and burgers.

Just out of curiosity, I asked around with a few other businesses in the strip mall. I popped into a mortgage office down the way, and asked about hauntings. "No," the lady behind the desk told me, "Nothing but good vibes in here." I then went to the largest building, which used to house a church my family attended. It now had the name "Wild Roots Preschool" on the front. I chatted with one of the teachers, a young brunette with long, straight hair, who was taking her coffee break. I mentioned the historic González Adobe next door.

"Oh yeah, it's super cute. We've been wanting to acquire it for our school. It's a shame it's just offices now; it's such a pretty building."

"Yeah, so much history here." I casually mentioned that I used to work at the restaurant next door, the old "Spunky Steer."

"Oh, that explains why some people call this the 'Spunky Steer Preschool.'"

"Did you know that restaurant was supposed to be haunted?"

"Oh, you've got to be kidding?" The teacher perked up. "*This* place is crazy haunted!"

She told me that at least ten different employees had seen strange things around the preschool. "It's sort of a running joke around here: the most haunted preschool in town. Things move around on their own. Doors open and shut. One employee actually even saw a full-bodied apparition, a person who wasn't even here."

It was common for teachers to respond to a "phantom cry." They would hear a child crying in a nearby room, and rush in to see if a child needed help. The room would be empty.

One teacher, Kelly, had one of the strangest experiences. Kelly had been visiting with students' parents, sitting at a table in the large playroom. Among the toys strewn about the floor lay a toy drum, wide and flat. The drum caught Kelly's eye. It slowly raised up above the ground, hovered in the air, then flew through a doorway into the adjacent room.

"Then Kelly heard a noise coming from that room. *Boom, boom, boom.* It was that toy drum. Someone was pounding it, this slow steady rhythm. *Boom, boom, boom.* It got louder and louder, more insistent. She and the parents got out of there without going to investigate."

I left late that evening, more than satisfied to learn that the ghosts were still around. Could the tales of a hangman's tree be true after all? I headed to the Temecula Valley Museum in search of answers.

Steve Williamson, a kindly museum employee in his sixties, agreed to tell me about the history of that strip mall on Jefferson. The old adobe building had been built in 1879 by José Gonzalez, and was one of the oldest still standing is southwestern Riverside County. José, a Basque man from Spain, was educated in Scotland as an accountant. He came to the area along with settler Juan Murrieta in the early 1870's, and built the house for his wife, Grace, and their children, Ormiston and Ysabel. I asked Steve if any other houses had stood near the González home.

"Not for a long time. It was just José and his family out there on the ranch."

"So there wasn't a hangman's tree next door to his house?" I asked.

Steve laughed. "Not likely! Only four people lived there. If they'd started hanging people, they would have run out of victims very soon."

Still, there had been human life there, on the site of the Sizzlin' Steer restaurant. Could that account for the ghosts? Steve explained that the González family weren't exactly the only people who had lived there. He told me the tragic story of Mercedes Pujol, who came to live at the adobe with them.

Mercedes was one of Temecula's prominent citizens in the Old West days. She was from Spain, where she had married Domingo Pujol, the owner of much of the land surrounding much of Temecula. After their wedding in Spain, Domingo moved back to California to manage his affairs, promising to send for his new bride. She was full of hope, with her whole bright future ahead of her.

Before the two could be reunited, however, just two years after their wedding, Domingo died.

Mercedes took a ship to California to settle Domingo's estate and manage his properties, which she inherited. When she came to Temecula, she met some of the other wealthy families of the area—including José González. Mercedes moved in with his family in that same adobe house, right next to where the steakhouse now stands, for several years.

While nobody was hanged on that site, there was plenty of sadness there. Mercedes was a woman in mourning, her future cut sadly short. She lived in the shadow of a happy, blossoming family, herself with no husband or children. All of that sadness has a way of sticking to a place. Sometimes, it may manifest itself as a haunting.

Many researchers describe hauntings as simple memories of the past, a sort of "cosmic replay" of past events that living humans perceive from time to time. One thing haunted places have in common is a sense of loss and tragedy, human suffering and intense emotion. Perhaps Mercedes' accumulated human suffering imprinted onto the place, a series of shadows of the past. Historical memories may still exist in our midst, restless shades not put to rest.

Whatever the explanation, something unusual definitely keeps manifesting here in this small shopping center on Jefferson Road. And yet, the Wild Roots Preschool certainly isn't the only Temecula school said to be haunted.

CHAPTER 3
The Ghost of the Math Building

Temecula Valley High School

The students sat quietly in the math classroom, finishing their exam. It was late October, and paper jack-o-lanterns decorated the windows. The teacher sat reading his book at the podium. Kelsey handed in her scantron sheet and asked for permission to use the restroom. The rest of the students continued to work in silence.

Suddenly, a scream rang out through the hallway.

The teacher stood from his chair and made a move for the classroom door. After a few seconds, he heard the muted thud of footsteps running toward him, down the padded hallway. The door slammed open and Kelsey stood panting, wide-eyed and pale.

"What's wrong?" the math teacher asked.

"I was in there and…" the student gasped. "I was all alone, and, and… The toilet flushed all by itself."

A few students laughed, but the teacher looked at her with complete seriousness. "You're not the first person to tell me that," he affirmed. "You see, there's a ghost in that bathroom."

* * * *

Temecula Valley High School was the first high school to be built in town. According to many people who have taught and studied there, the math building is extremely haunted.

The math classrooms are located in Building 14, a U-shaped structure to the right of the campus's main entrance. An indoor carpeted hallway runs the length of Building 14, with rows of classrooms on either side. A few wood-paneled skylights illuminate this hallway during the day. I still recall the ethereal glow of the natural light that filtered through those skylights in the late afternoon, casting long black shadows on the carpet.

I first heard of the ghosts from my math teacher, Dave Dempster. Whenever we had a free moment at the end of math class, Dempster would share the stories that he had heard over the years. While the entire math building was haunted, he told us, the activity was heaviest in the girls' restroom, on the opposite end of the building.

Some of his most noteworthy tales had been told by school custodians who worked in Building 14 during the quiet evening hours, when everyone else had left for the day. These are three of the experiences they shared with Dempster.

Story #1: The Doors

A custodian was working late one afternoon cleaning the classrooms, when he heard the distant sound of a door opening and closing. He recognized the noise made by the metallic push-bar on the dual doors that led to the exterior patio. Someone had opened the doors on the opposite end of the building, at the other tip of the "U-shape," out of the janitor's sight.

Assuming that it might be a teacher who needed something, he paused his work and walked down the length of the hall. By the time he reached the glass doors at the other end of the building, nobody was there. He peered through the tinted glass and saw a vast, empty patio outside, with no sign of another soul.

At that moment, he heard the patio doors open on the *other* side of the building, where he had just been working a minute ago. He quickly walked back to the other end of the U, but again found nothing. He picked up a bottle of cleaning solution, prepared to get back to work—and again, he heard the doors slam shut on the other side of the building.

He raced around to the other end; surely, he would catch up to the person who was opening these doors. Still, the hallway and the patio were entirely empty. Whoever was doing this, they defied the laws of the material world.

Story #2: The Hands

This happened to a female custodian; let's just call her "Sharon." While she continued to work at this high school for years after her experience, she refused to ever clean the math building again.

Sharon was all alone in here one evening, vacuuming one of the classrooms at the far end, down by the bathrooms. She suddenly felt two hands pressing down on her shoulders. She whipped around, startled—nobody was there.

She continued to vacuum, and once again felt those hands pressing down on her. Instinctively, she raised a hand to knock the person's arm away, but felt nothing but empty space behind her.

Sharon left work immediately. A very religious woman, she raced home, pulled her Bible out with shaking hands, and read from the Psalms. Once she had calmed down enough, she felt brave enough to confront the unseen presence. Tossing her Bible into her handbag, she grabbed a bottle of holy water and headed back to campus. She returned to the same classroom, sprinkled holy water throughout, and read from the Bible out loud. The entire time, she half expected to feel those heavy hands pressing down again on her shoulders. Thankfully, though, they left her alone for the rest of the night.

Still, Sharon refused to ever work in Building 14 again. If those spirits ever showed up again, somebody else could exorcize them the next time.

Story #3: The Woman in White

"Mark" had heard the ghost stories from his fellow custodians. He always listened quietly, never quite sure what to believe. One evening, he decided to put the tales to the test. After he finished up work for the day, he decided to post up in the hallway of the math building. He would sit there and wait, to matter how long it took. If there were any ghosts here, he was determined to see them for himself.

Mark dragged a chair into the carpeted hallway and positioned it in front of the door to classroom number 1408, right at the corner of the building's U-shape. This would allow him to see all the way down the hall on both ends. He sat there and waited, read a paperback novel in the dim light, and periodically glancing up both ends of the hall.

After about an hour, as Mark was staring down toward the doors leading to the outside patio, something caught his eye in the opposite hall. He turned and gasped.

An unmistakably human figure had appeared.

Mark hadn't seen where she came from. She seemed to just emerge from out of the wall, down at the far end of the hallway. Mark described her as "an Indian woman in a white flowing dress." There was a filmy, translucent look to her body. "How else could I describe her?" Mark said. "She looked exactly like what you'd expect a ghost to look like."

The woman in white walked slowly down the dark hallway, toward the corner where Mark sat. He remained absolutely still. The woman walked resolutely onward, appearing not to notice him. When she reached the wall to his left, she walked straight through it. "It was like she just melted right into the wall, right into room 1408."

Mark stood from his chair and walked away, towards the exit doors. When he was about to leave the building, he saw the same woman in white emerge from the wall and step back into the hallway, about 80 feet away from him.

This time, however, she paused. She turned toward Mark and locked eyes with him. Then she dissolved into darkness.

* * * *

What is it about school bathrooms that seems to attract ghost stories? As far back as elementary school, I heard tales of "Bloody Mary" appearing in our bathroom mirror. Students around the world have told similar stories.

Just north of Temecula, the University of California at Riverside has its own bathroom ghost. In the Tomas Rivera Library on the main campus, a spirit haunts the restroom on the third floor. The lights will often turn on and off on their own, and the ghost occasionally touches people in the stalls. They say it is the vengeful spirit of a graduate student who committed suicide.

Back at TVHS, meanwhile, Dave Dempster never offered an explanation for why the math building was haunted. He simply knew that it was, and was always happy to share these ghost stories with his class. One afternoon as he was doing so, a female student asked for permission to go check out the "bathroom ghost" for herself.

"Sure you can," Dempster said with a smile. "I doubt you'll see anything; it's not like ghosts perform on command or anything. But just in case, you'd better bring a friend with you. She can be your witness. Also, you might feel a little safer with someone else there."

The two girls walked down the hallway as Dempster chatted with the other students. After a couple of minutes, the girls burst back into the classroom, panting and chattering excitedly.

"Whoa, whoa!" Dempster said. "Calm down there! What happened?"

"We went into the bathroom," one girl said. "And checked all the stalls. They were all empty. We were about to come back, when… All the toilets flushed at the same time."

* * * *

Dave Dempster continued to teach math at TVHS for years after I graduated, finally retiring in 2019. When I contacted him recently to refresh my memory, he told me another strange detail about room 1408.

This classroom was larger than the others, and had been equipped as a computer lab. Given its convenient size, the math teachers would eat lunch there nearly every day, sitting at the two long tables in the middle of the room. Directly underneath these tables, the teachers noticed, there was an unusual acoustic dead zone.

"If you banged the heel of your shoe against the floor directly under those tables," Dempster told me, "it made a very different sound than anywhere else in that room, or any other room in the building, for that matter. That section sounded strangely hollow." Nobody could ever find a physical explanation for this strange sound.

My friend Amy Hoak attended TVHS at the same time as me. Years later, she returned to campus as a substitute teacher. "I *bet* that building is haunted!" She commented. "There's a weird vibe about that entire side of campus. Something about it is just… I don't know… Energetically *dense*."

Amy also pointed out that the building's number, 14, has a particular significance in the tradition of numerology. As "the number of karmic debt," unresolved issues and improper actions are said to be "held" in the number 14. Another interesting point: in Japanese culture, the numeral 4 is considered bad luck. The Japanese name for four, "*shi*," is pronounced the same as the word for "death."

It is also worth pointing out that Stephen King wrote a short story about a cursed hotel room, later made into a feature film starring John Cusack. The number of that room: 1408. The number on the classroom with the oddly hollow-sounding floor, the room from which the ghostly woman in white emerged. Coincidence? Or does this number somehow attract negativity, unusual energy, or strange activity?

When I recently spoke with Dave Dempster, he still had no clear idea of why the building was haunted. He did recall, however, that the custodian had described the ghostly woman in white as a Native American. "I've heard claims of 'Indian burial grounds' around the campus," Dempster said, "but this is a common attribution, and I cannot corroborate it."

There is no telling how many burial sites may lie beneath Temecula, unmarked and forgotten by time. Given how many Luiseño settlements were in the valley for thousands of years before European contact, any given building may stand atop an old burial ground. That might explain the strange phenomena I heard about from one gas station on Temecula Parkway.

CHAPTER 4
The Gas Station Poltergeist

Corner of Margarita Road and Temecula Parkway

I stopped into the Arco gas station just minutes after the ghost appeared. I just barely missed her.

I had been researching legends in Old Town one warm summer evening in 2020. Old Town was the place you would expect to find ghosts, after all. As I was about to leave town, I stopped for gas at the Arco on the corner of Margarita Road and Temecula Parkway. Two employees chatted with each other behind the counter of the convenience store, a young man and middle-aged woman.

"I saw her again tonight, Cindy," the young man said. "I'm telling you, this place is haunted as shit."

My ears perked up. Trying to avoid being too obvious about my eavesdropping, I nonchalantly walked over to the magazine rack and picked up a periodical to flip through. Cindy stared at me. She noticed that I was holding the copy of *Bridal Monthly* upside down.

"Uh… Can I help you?" she said.

"Sorry, I just overheard you guys talking about hauntings."

"Oh, sure. We've got a resident ghost here."

I turned to her younger coworker. "What did you mean when you said you saw 'her' again?"

"Oh, it was freaky as shit," the young man said. "Just before you came in, I looked over in that back corner and saw a woman standing there, with her back to me."

He pointed toward the far corner of the convenience store, far away from the entrance door.

"I assumed it was Cindy. But then I realized, she had just gone into the back room. *What's she doing out here now,* I thought, *standing in the aisles?* I leaned over and looked into the back storage room. Sure enough, there was Cindy, doing inventory. I turned back to the woman in the aisles, but… *Poof.* She's gone. Vanished into thin air."

Cindy nodded as her coworker told the story. "Also, things fall off the shelves all the time," she told me.

I tried to play the part of skeptic. "Well, how do you know the merchandise isn't just arranged in an awkward position?"

"That *would* make sense," she told me. "If it were just stuff falling down off the racks. But look over there… You see that freezer?"

She pointed to the transparent glass door of the refrigerated section. A grave expression appeared on her face.

"Sometimes, there will be something that just catches my eye over there. I look over and see things sliding around *inside* the cooler. Pints of ice cream moving around on their own, sliding back and forth right in the front of the racks. Like someone is picking them up and rearranging them."

"We're used to it by now," the young man said. "But neither of us ever works a shift alone. You've always got to have a buddy with you. 'Cause even if you don't… You know you're never alone."

This gas station happens to be located near one of the oldest settlements from Temecula's Old West days. Vail Ranch was a trading post dating back to 1844, when Pablo Apis purchased the land. The store built there by Louis Wolf is one of the oldest adobes still standing. Maybe all that history has something to do with the phenomena in the gas station. Then again, it might also be related to the fact that the gas station is just a short distance down the road from an unmarked mass grave.

CHAPTER 5
The Temecula Massacre

Location undisclosed

Over a hundred people died in that violent, bloody massacre. Their mass grave lies right in the middle of a modern shopping center. When I first heard of this place, it sounded like the perfect location for ghost stories.

I was wrong.

It would be impossible to write this book without acknowledging the Temecula Massacre and the burial site of its victims. Of all the historic spots in Temecula Valley, this cemetery has likely attracted the most attention of local "ghost hunters."

It is also the one that they should leave alone.

As I dug deep into the history behind the massacre and the final resting place of its victims, I found a sobering, somber lesson in tragedy. While it involves a horrific chapter in Temecula's history, this is not your typical ghost story.

The History of the Temecula Massacre

I will not reveal the precise location of the burial ground, for reasons that will become clear later on. While it is easy enough to locate through research, I would like to ask every reader to please show restraint. Before you go looking for this place, please read all the way to the end of the chapter.

The cemetery does not provide much to look at. An unremarkable brown wall surrounds it, the cement molded to look like old adobe bricks. The burial ground itself is a simple, square plot of land in the middle of a suburban parking lot. When I peered over the top of the wall, I saw nothing but dirt and weeds inside. No grave markers, no signs, no plaques of any sort.

Nothing that would suggest the tragic, bloody history behind this cemetery.

The Temecula Massacre occurred in the year 1847, in a canyon near what is now the Vail Dam. A group of Cahuilla warriors lured their Temecula-Luiseño rivals into the canyon and slaughtered them by the dozens. For much of Temecula's history, many locals simply thought the massacre was a battle between two warring groups of Native people. While it is true that different communities occasionally fought each, the real story of this massacre stretches much further. It is a tragic tale of war by proxy, with two groups of Natives manipulated into fighting someone else's fight.

In order to understand the Temecula Massacre, we need to understand an earlier event known as the Pauma Massacre. And to understand that, we must first understand the broader context: the Mexican-American War.

By late 1846, it was still unclear which side would win the war: the Mexican soldiers defending Alta California, or the invading forces from the United States. After the Battle of San Pasqual in December, both sides claimed victory. (The San Pasqual battlefield near Escondido is itself a famously haunted spot.) After the battle, a group of Mexican soldiers withdrew to a ranch at the nearby Pauma Valley to regroup.

This was the point when both sides—the U.S. and Mexican factions—pulled Native groups into the fight.

One group of local Luiseño people were sympathetic toward the Americans, perhaps hoping that they would fare better under U.S. occupation than Mexican occupation. By some accounts, an American named Bill Marshall helped to convince them. Marshall had a personal bone to pick with one of the Mexican soldiers (José María Alvarado had married the woman

Marshall loved), and Marshall seized the occasion to encourage the Luiseños to take up arms against Mexico's soldiers.

Luiseño warriors laid siege to the ranch at Pauma and held the Mexicans captive. Tensions rose and the situation became increasingly messy, with chiefs of multiple communities debating what to do. Accusations arose that the Mexican forces had stolen horses from the Luiseños. Eventually, the tensions broiled over—all eleven Mexican men were killed. This event, known as the Pauma Massacre, is described by Herbert Lockwood in his excellent 1967 book, *Fallout from the Skeleton's Closet: A Light Look at San Diego History*.

Mexican General José María Flores called for retaliation. When he heard of the slaughter, Flores gave orders to avenge the men's deaths. The Luiseños would pay with blood, and the dirty work would be done by a different group of Native fighters: the Cahuilla, people who were friendly with the Mexican forces.

Under the command of Mexican officer José del Carmen Lugo, the Cahuilla warriors went looking for the Luiseños in the Temecula area. In January 1847, Mexican and Cahuilla forces surprised the Luiseños and lured them into a canyon. Once they had the Luiseños trapped, they slaughtered them mercilessly.

Accounts from the period describe the canyon as being littered with dead bodies for weeks after the massacre. Heavy rains made it impossible to go back into the canyon and retrieve them, and many Luiseños were afraid of further attacks. By the time the Mormon Battalion marched through the area in late January, they witnessed the aftermath.

George Cook was marching westward with the Mormon Battalion when he came across a group of bloodied and bedraggled Native people limping along the path. The survivors carried several bodies, and begged for help burying their dead. Cook and his companions refused and continued on their way. As they moved on, they began to notice other bodies scattered along the road. Eventually, they came across a group of Native people marching in single file, singing and beating drums. It was a funeral procession, maintaining tradition in the midst of horror.

The aftershocks of these battles lasted for years after the Treaty of Guadalupe Hidalgo was signed, with recurring waves of retaliatory killings throughout this region. All that death and tragedy—and all to fight for other people's interests.

The Temecula Massacre was a proxy war: two groups set against each other to defend others' interests. No matter who won, the Native people would lose.

How many wars throughout human history could be described in the same terms? Quite a few of them. The elite hire poor working people to fight for their economic and political interests. "Rich man's war, poor man's fight," as the saying goes. The soldiers in most human wars have more in common with each other than they do with those whose interests they defend. The history of the Temecula Massacre is a microcosm of centuries of human bloodshed, brother pitted against brother.

This tragic and violent tale ends at the graveyard. The victims of the massacre were finally buried, by their loved ones, in a graveyard in Temecula. While all grave markers have rotted away, the cemetery still stands, unceremoniously engulfed by a shopping center.

Searching for ghosts

Like many people, I grew up hearing tales of haunted houses that were built on top of a Native American burial ground. It remains a common trope in horror movies. The first Halloween-themed episode of *The Simpsons*, "The Treehouse of Horror," parodied this theme: when the family discovers an "Indian burial ground" beneath their home, one of the tombstones reads, "Gandhi."

Perhaps because I grew up hearing these stories, the cemetery in Temecula sounded like the perfect spot for a haunting. I decided to go and investigate.

Initially, I hoped to hike into the very canyon where the fighting had taken place. This proved impossible, at least without some scuba gear—the whole canyon is now underwater. When Vail Dam was built, it flooded the canyon, creating Vail Lake. (This is probably for the best, since the original name for that canyon contains a racial epithet I'd rather not put into print.)

It was possible to go visit the cemetery, though. As I walked by the brown, faux adobe wall, I wondered why there were no signs or markers of any kind. Why had nobody installed a memorial plaque to remember the dead?

I inquired at all the nearby businesses, including a supermarket, a barber shop, pet store, restaurant, and a gym. I came up empty in every place: not a single ghost story to be found. In fact, at all those locations, only one employee had even *heard* of the graveyard, and only in vague terms. "Oh yeah," she said, "I know there's a graveyard there, but I don't know any of the history." Everyone else just went about their business in this modern Southern California strip mall, oblivious to the bones of the past.

It wasn't until I stopped into a bar adjacent to the cemetery that I finally found a few ghost stories. However, none of them were directly linked to the burial ground. When I asked a blonde waitress in her 20s about ghosts, she casually told me that she had "seen spirits."

"Really? Here?" I asked. "In this bar, or near the graveyard?"

"No, not here. At my house down the road. I woke up one night and saw a full, shadowy figure hovering over me. A second later, I felt someone lie down next to me. I rolled over, and I could see the blankets and the mattress depress in the shape of a human body. That wasn't the only time, either."

"Wow. But you've never seen spirits in here?"

"I won't give them the chance! People tell me it's a gift to be able to see these things, but I don't *want* to see them. So I refuse to work late nights here." She glanced at the window, towards the parking lot and the cemetery wall. "Who knows what I might come across."

Another young waitress told me that she used to live in a haunted house in Temecula, near Chelsea Way. She was ten years old when she and her family moved in, and they only lasted a year there. "I remember playing in my room, and I would suddenly get the chills. I always felt like there was someone watching me. We'd hear strange creaks and noises all the time."

"Well, that can happen in a lot of old houses…" I began.

"Also, the porch fell off."

"The, uh… Pardon?"

"The porch broke off the house. My mom was standing on it when it happened! She had to jump into the house to keep from falling down with it. It had never given any warning, it just fell right off one day. And later on, we learned that the house had been built on an old graveyard."

Just goes to show you, the ghost stories don't always pop up where you expect. I had come expecting stories about the cemetery, but heard more tales of hauntings in ordinary places in suburban Temecula. What of the unmarked cemetery, though? Had anyone experienced anything remotely "paranormal" there?

A quick internet search brought up a YouTube video by a group of local ghost hunters, known as the "Soul Seekers," who hopped the wall and filmed inside the cemetery. The video was less than impressive.

One of the young men introduces the video by saying, "Tonight, we're here to approve or disprove a haunting." An on-screen caption appears at this point, claiming that a ghostly mist is visible. (Meanwhile, I was distracted by the fact that the host seemed to think the word "approve" was the opposite of "disprove.")

The three ghost hunters walk around the cemetery, trying to communicate with the dead Native Americans through their digital recorders. They set up flashlights and insist that the spirits turn them on to prove their presence. While the video caption claims to have captured "a full body [sic] apparition," I saw nothing more than refracted light from the nearby highway. The host ends his visit by speaking directly to the spirits: "We're gonna leave your location here. We didn't vandalize it [...] We didn't destroy any of your property, so please stay here. Don't follow us home."

Despite the ghost hunters' insistence that they came "with respect," the whole video left a bad taste in my mouth. Watching it disabused me of my own ideas about sneaking into the cemetery some night. Something about the entire spectacle felt invasive and forced.

I couldn't help but wonder what Temecula's modern-day Native residents thought of all this. The descendants of those people laid to rest in this cemetery, the Pechanga Band of Luiseño Indians, had the ultimate say on this cemetery and how it should be treated. What was their opinion? I headed out to the Pechanga Reservation to search for answers.

Honoring the Ancestors

After asking around the reservation, I finally managed to contact Myra Masiel-Zamora, M.A., Curator with the Pechanga Tribal Historic Preservation Office. I spoke with her over the phone and asked about the cemetery and the history of the massacre. She told me, with a discernible sigh, that I wasn't the first outsider interested in this place. As she discussed it, one word came up repeatedly: "hurtful."

Myra told me that she was familiar with the groups of "ghost hunters" who had trespassed on the cemetery grounds, taking videos and recordings. She had even heard rumors of some tour companies who brought their customers to the site in the past. The fact that these tours were for-profit operations added insult to injury.

"To think that there are people out there who actually profit from this, who see it as a chance to make money… Well, it's extremely hurtful. We've asked them to respect our ancestors, to simply leave them alone."

This was an appeal to basic common sense and decency: any cemetery should be treated with respect. Nobody's beloved ancestors are a tourist attraction. An additional dimension, in the case of this particular cemetery, was its connection to so much violence and tragedy. The idea of traipsing about this hallowed ground trying to record "Electronic Voice Phenomena" felt extremely disrespectful—obscene, even. It reminded me of news stories of tourists who had recently walked around Auschwitz to play "Pokémon Go" on their phones. (Yes, that really happened.)

When I told Myra that I was researching the Temecula Massacre for a book about hauntings, she made one point very clear: this cemetery is not a place for ghost stories. "To be frank, it's quite hurtful to hear people describe our ancestors as 'ghosts.' The very use of the word 'ghost' is hurtful. We don't view our ancestors in that way; we have a very different worldview. We have a deep connection to this land. We have been here for thousands of years, since the world was created. Our ancestors are to be revered and respected. They are not 'ghosts.'"

Finally, I asked her why the site remained unmarked. Many people I had talked to thought a memorial or a plaque would be appropriate. Had the Tribal authorities ever talked of setting up some sort of historical marker? Would such a sign perhaps encourage respect for the cemetery?

"Just the opposite—I feel like a sign would only make things worse. People would go poking around there even more frequently."

What would be the best approach, then?

"We would prefer to simply not attract attention to it. We've had problems with vandalism already. We've talked about building a better fence to prevent trespassing, but it's been difficult during the pandemic."

She left me with one final, sobering observation: this was not the only unmarked grave site in the area. Far from it.

"There are cemeteries like that all over the valley. In fact, anywhere you see a plot of land fenced off, set aside… It's likely another place where our ancestors are buried. And we treat it just like we treat any cemetery: with respect and reverence."

Myra's comments served as a somber reminder that some wounds of the past are still painfully raw. In addition, there are many different ways to honor the dead. While many Western cultures prefer to put up a plaque or monument, the Indigenous people of Temecula Valley remember the people who died in this tragedy with respectful silence.

This conversation also reminded me that some tragedies are to be contemplated from a healthy distance. As I've discussed in the preceding chapters, pain and suffering often lie behind ghost stories and haunted places. As we explore these stories, however, we must also establish certain limits. In thinking about the Temecula Massacre, I thought of a much more recent tale of suffering in this valley: the case of the Turpin family in Perris, CA.

Over the course of several years, David Allen Turpin and Louise Anna Turpin imprisoned their thirteen children in a literal house of horrors. The children were chained, beaten, and subjected to unspeakable abuse, all inside an everyday suburban home in Perris. They were only freed when one of the Turpin daughters managed to escape and dial 9-1-1.

Now, from a "paranormal" point of view, it's likely that all that pain and suffering left an imprint on the house. There may be some sort of unique psychic energy or unusual phenomena left behind. But does that mean we should go poking around that house? Should we sneak in with Geiger counters, EVP recorders, and "ghost hunter" apps? Not if we have any sense of human decency. We should respect the survivors' privacy and let them heal on their own.

On this somber note, I have one final request for all readers: please, I beg of you, do not go poking around the cemetery of the Temecula Massacre. Let us respect the wishes of the Pechanga Band of Luiseño Indians, the original people of this valley, and treat that site with the reverence that it deserves. It is not a tourist attraction or a "ghost hunting" site. It is a revered cemetery, one that is linked to an extremely tragic chapter in local history.

If you do happen to pass by the unmarked cemetery, please be respectful of the dead who lie there. Don't hop the fence to take cheap videos there. The police have been alerted of the issue, and will not hesitate to prosecute trespassers. Simply pay your respects, take off your hat, say a quick prayer, and move on. Let us all remember to honor those who were here long before us, here on this ancient land.

* * * *

This first collection of stories is just the tip of the iceberg. The entire Temecula Valley is rich with chilling and haunting tales, not all of which are ghost stories. As we continue through this series, we will find tales of mysterious creatures, strange natural phenomena, and enigmatic lights in the sky.

The further we dig, the more questions we uncover. Join me in this exploration of the profound mysteries of this haunted desert valley.

Coming soon…

Book Two in the "Haunted Temecula Valley" series:

Haunted Roadways

When a driver starts heading downhill toward the bridge, the driver will notice what looks like a pedestrian standing in the road. As the headlights draw closer to the figure, however, it becomes clear that this is no ordinary person. The limbs are too long, the neck extended, the gait is uncanny. The figure could better be described as "human-like."

As the vehicle approaches, the figure runs across the road at an unnatural speed. Then it suddenly disappears, seemingly into thin air.

The strange thing is, deep water and marsh lie on either side of the road. If a human were running across the road at full speed, they would drop into the water with a splash. Of course, something not entirely human might navigate the landscape more easily. It might not mind jumping into the water. If some creature lives in the area, could it be related to the strange deaths that occurred?

Stay tuned!

For more information on the series, see:
www.HolyGhostStories.com

Bibliography

Introduction

A Thousand Years in Temecula Valley.
Tom Hudson, 1982.

CHAPTER TWO

Interview with Steve Williamson, Temecula Valley Museum.

CHAPTER THREE

The Field Guide to Southern California Hauntings.
Nicole Strickland. Ghost Research Society. 2009.

CHAPTER FIVE

Fallout from the Skeleton's Closet: A Light Look at San Diego History.
Herbert Lockwood. 1967.

https://www.youtube.com/watch?v=ZMR_1KWxXNw
Soul Seekers At The Haunted Temecula Massacre Site and Unmarked Indian Burial Ground
 Apr 10, 2012

Interview with
Myra Masiel-Zamora, M.A., Curator with the Pechanga Tribal Historic Preservation Office

https://www.temeculaca.gov/155/Temecula-Massacre
Temecula Massacre.

ABOUT THE AUTHOR

David J. Schmidt is an author, podcaster, multilingual translator, and homebrewer who splits his time between Mexico City and San Diego, California.

Schmidt has published a variety of books, short stories, and articles in English and Spanish. His English-language titles include such works of "non-fiction horror" as ***Three Nights in the Clown Motel***, and ***Holy Ghosts: True Tales from a Haunted Christian College***, as well as *The Tiny Staircase series,* devoted to the mysterious and the unexplained. His Spanish-language books ***Más frío que la nieve: cuentos sobrenaturales de Rusia*** and ***Tunguska: luces en el cielo sobre Siberia*** were published nationwide in Mexico.

Schmidt is the co-host of the podcast *To Russia with Love.* He speaks twelve languages and has been to 33 countries. He received his B.A. in psychology from Point Loma Nazarene University.

Website: www.holyghoststories.com
Amazon:
https://www.amazon.com/David-J.-Schmidt/e/B00BXTBY7K
Facebook: @HolyGhostStories
YouTube: Holy Ghosts
Twitter: @SchmidtTales